DARKEST DEPTHS AND OTHER UNDERGROUND MEGASTRUCTURES

Ian Graham

QED Publishing

Created for QED Publishing by Tall Tree Ltd
www.talltreebooks.co.uk
Editor: Rob Colson
Designers: Malcolm Parchment and Jonathan Vipond
Illustrations: Apple Illustration and Caroline Watson

First published in the UK in 2011 by
QED Publishing
A Quarto Group company
226 City Road
London EC1V 2TT

www.qed-publishing.co.uk

A catalogue record for this book is available from the British Library.

ISBN-978 1 84835 656 6

Printed in China

Picture credits
(t=top, b=bottom, l=left, r=right, c=centre, fc=front cover)
Alamy fc David R. Frazier Photolibrary, Inc.,6t Doug Steley, 10t Danita Delimont, 15 Tom Tracy Photography, 18l QA Photos.com, 27l Ady Kerry; **Bill Ebbesen** 17c; **BP** 24l; 24–25; **Corbis** 5b Paull A Souders, 8–9 Staff/Reuters, 11b Peter Andrews/Reuters, 12 Cezaro de Luca/epa, 13t Nadeem Khawer/epa, 18l Pascal Rossignol/Reuters, 18r Jacques Langevin/Sygma, 20–21 Najla Feanny, 20t Tom Fox/Dallas Morning News, 23r George Steinmetz, 26l Stefan Wermuth/Reuters; **Dreamstime** 23l Natalia Bratslavsky; **Eurotunnel** 19t; **Getty** 5t Joe Raedle, 13b Hulton Archive, 19r AFP/Denis Charlet; **Gump Stump** 6–7; **iStock** 9b Eduard Andras, 28–29 Robas; **Markus Schweiss** 10–11; **Photolibarary** 7 The Print Collector; **Risto Kaijaluoto** 17; **Shutterstock** 4 Arnold John Labrentz, 14–15 Lee Prince, 21t Kola-Kola, 27r Natalia Bratslavsky; **US Government** 25t

Words in **bold** are explained in the Glossary on page 32.

Contents

Digging down

Deep holes are dug in the ground to get at fossil fuels such as coal and oil. Deep tunnels may be excavated to dispose safely of dangerous materials such as the **radioactive** waste from nuclear power stations. Tunnels also allow cars or trains to travel underneath mountains or seas.

Mining

Mines are dug to bring valuable and useful materials up from deep underground. Most of these materials are part of the rock itself. Rock is made of **minerals**, and some minerals contain the metals and other substances that we want to use. These minerals are called ores. Mines are dug down to reach the rock that contains the valuable ores.

Drilling

Coal and minerals have to be cut out of the ground, but oil and gas will come to the surface by themselves. If a hole is drilled down to oil and gas trapped underground, the pressure will squirt them all the way up to the surface. Scientists drill holes in the ground to bring up samples of earth, rock and ice for research. Water pumped down drill-holes can be heated by hot rocks deep underground. When the hot water comes back up to the surface, the heat can be used to warm buildings or to make electricity.

▲ *Oil workers connect a pipe to the drill in order to collect oil that is forced to the surface from deep underground.*

Tunnelling

Deep tunnels allow cars and trains to pass underneath mountains, rivers and even the sea. Deep tunnels are also used to store dangerous substances. Nuclear reactors produce waste that cannot be thrown away like ordinary rubbish because it is radioactive. This means that it gives out dangerous rays and particles. One way to deal with it is to store it in deep tunnels. The Waste Isolation Pilot Plant in New Mexico, USA, stores radioactive waste in underground tunnels 650 metres below the surface.

▲ *Drums full of radioactive waste arrive at the bottom of a shaft 650 metres underground in the Waste Isolation Pilot Plant in New Mexico.*

▼ *The tunnels in mines are big enough for mechanical diggers, drilling machines and even trains to fit inside.*

Deep challenges

The immense pressure deep underground creates a lot of difficulties for deep digging or drilling. Rock can fly out of a mine's walls, oil and gas can erupt from a well like lava from a volcano, and tunnels can cave in as they are being dug

▼ *In April 2010, an underwater blow-out caused the Deepwater Horizon oil rig in the Gulf of Mexico to explode.*

Rock burst

Rock at great depths underground is squashed by the weight of all the ground above it. When a deep mine is dug, the huge weight pressing down on it can make rock explode out of its walls. Called **rock burst**, it is a great danger in the world's deepest mines.

◄ *In deep mines, rock that looks dangerous, perhaps because it is cracked, can be covered with steel mesh or blown out with explosives before it bursts.*

Blow-outs

Oil and gas trapped deep underground are under tremendous pressure. When an **oil well** is drilled, the oil or gas cannot be allowed to gush out of the top of the well. A safety valve called a **blow-out** preventer is fitted to the top of a well. If oil or gas tries to gush out – an emergency called a blow-out – the blow-out preventer seals the well.

Cave-ins

Tunnelling near rivers or the sea is dangerous because the soft ground can cave in. In the 19th century, the **tunnelling shield** was invented to solve this problem. The shield was an iron frame as big as the tunnel, and it held up the walls and roof while the tunnellers dug. Then the whole frame was pushed forwards, the newly dug part of the tunnel was lined with bricks, and tunnelling continued. Modern tunnelling machines still have a shield to prevent the tunnels from caving in.

▶ *The tunnelling shield held up a tunnel's roof while the men inside it dug the tunnel.*

MEGA FACTS

In 2008, an underground railway tunnel being dug in China collapsed, and a hole 75 metres across opened up in the road above it.

Tunnelling deep

Digging a deep tunnel involves cutting through solid rock. This work used to be done by hand, but today, giant machines usually do it. Until the 1960s, tunnels were dug by using handheld drills, explosives, picks and shovels. It was a long, slow process and very hard work. Today, most long, deep tunnels are built by tunnel boring machines (TBMs).

Boring machines

The TBMs used today are as big as the tunnels they make. The front of the machine is a disc called the cutter head, which is covered with rows of teeth made of a very tough metal called tungsten carbide. The cutter head rotates slowly, about once every 10–15 seconds, and the teeth cut through the rock. The rock, now called spoil, falls onto a conveyor belt inside the TBM. The moving belt carries the spoil to the back of the machine, where a train takes it away to the surface. Meanwhile, the TBM moves forwards and pushes the rotating cutter head against the rock.

Lining

Whichever construction method is used, the tunnel is then lined. In the past, tunnels were lined with bricks. Today, they are usually lined with concrete blocks. The blocks are bigger and stronger than bricks, and also faster to put in place.

▼ TBMs can tunnel through soft and hard rock, but if the rock is too hard, explosives are used instead.

MEGA FACTS

The biggest TBMs are almost 16 metres in diameter. With all the back-up systems that trail behind them, they can be 250 metres long.

▶ *A TBM is controlled by an operator inside the machine. The operator steers by pushing the cutter head forwards more on one side than the other.*

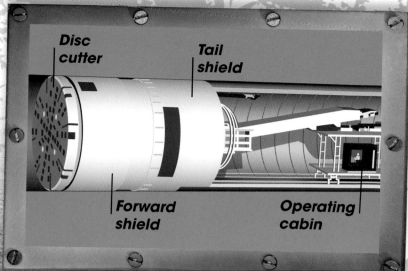

Disc cutter

Tail shield

Forward shield

Operating cabin

Blasting holes

When a tunnel needs to be dug using explosives, holes several metres deep are first dug into the rock using a machine called a drilling jumbo. The holes are filled with explosives and the rock is blasted out, making the tunnel a little longer. The process is then repeated.

▲ *A drilling jumbo has a number of drills at the ends of long mechanical arms to drill deep holes.*

Mining for minerals

The surface of the Earth is made of rock, which contains minerals made of useful materials such as metals. Minerals and other materials, such as coal, are cut from the ground by mining. If minerals are near the surface, they can be reached by removing the earth above them. This is called open-cast mining. If they are deeper underground, shafts are dug down to them and tunnels dug out sideways from the shafts.

◀ A miner places explosives in holes drilled into the wall of a zinc and silver mine.

▲ A longwall shearer moves back and forth along a coalface cutting out the coal.

Mining methods

When miners started digging deep mines, they had to find a way to stop the roof falling in on them. One of the methods they used is called room and pillar. Chambers called rooms were dug out, leaving pillars of rock between them to hold up the roof. The room-and-pillar method is still used in salt mines today.

Coal is mined using a method called longwall mining. A line of props up to 400 metres long, called powered roof supports, holds up the roof. A machine called a shearer moves along the line of roof supports with whirling cutters, tearing out the coal. The coal falls onto a conveyor belt, which carries it away. While the shearer cuts the coal, other machines dig the mine's tunnels.

Mining rare minerals

The longwall mining method cannot be used to mine rare minerals and metals such as gold. There is not enough gold in one place to make it worthwhile using the huge machines used in coal mining, and the rock in gold mines is also too hard for them. Instead, the rock is shattered by explosives.

▲ *Miners use hand-held drills to dig into the rock face in the Western Deep gold mine in South Africa, which is 2500 metres deep.*

MEGA FACTS

During your lifetime, you will use about 14,800 kilograms of iron, 12,800 kilograms of salt and 360 kilograms of lead — most of which is dug out from mines.

Working underground

Mining is one of the world's most dangerous jobs. The hazards miners face deep underground include fires, explosions and cave-ins. Big, powerful machines are used in small spaces close to workers, the tunnels and shafts are difficult to escape from in an emergency, and dangerous gases can build up inside a mine.

Collapse in Chile

On 5 August 2010, part of the San José mine in Chile collapsed. For 17 days, nobody knew if the miners were dead or alive. Then a probe lowered down a hole came back up with a note attached. It said that all 33 miners were alive, but they were trapped 622 metres below the surface. A shaft was drilled down to them and a specially built rescue capsule, called Phoenix, was lowered down the shaft to bring up the miners, one by one. By the time they were rescued, they had been trapped underground for more than two months.

◄ Miners trapped in the San José mine were rescued using the Phoenix. The capsule was big enough for just one person to get inside.

Fire and explosion

When the ground is disturbed by digging, gases are released. These include flammable gases such as methane, which can catch fire or explode. Mines have to be **ventilated**, using special ventilation tunnels, to stop these gases building up to dangerous levels.

▲ *Coal miners in Pakistan use wooden beams to secure the roof of the mine.*

Heat and air

The deeper you dig into the ground, the hotter it is. The rising temperature as you go deeper underground is called the **geothermal gradient.** Because of the geothermal gradient, the deepest mines are very hot. At a depth of 3660 metres, the walls of a mine can be as hot as 65 degrees Celsius. Miners are able to work only if cool air is blown through the mine.

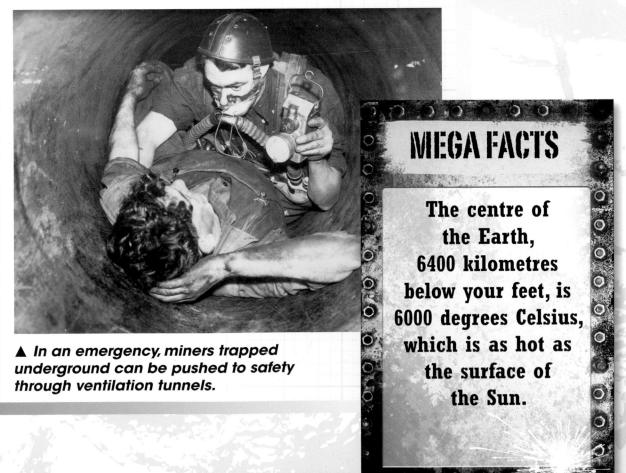

▲ *In an emergency, miners trapped underground can be pushed to safety through ventilation tunnels.*

MEGA FACTS

The centre of the Earth, 6400 kilometres below your feet, is 6000 degrees Celsius, which is as hot as the surface of the Sun.

The Bingham Canyon Mine is an open-cast mine near Salt Lake City in Utah, USA. More than a kilometre deep already, and getting deeper by the day, it is the world's deepest open-cast mine.

The rock that is mined at the Bingham Canyon Mine contains copper ore, which is a mineral from which the metal copper can be extracted. The rock also contains smaller amounts of silver, gold and platinum. Surrounding the mine are grinding mills, a smelter and a refinery, where the metals are extracted from the rock and ores.

MEGA FACTS

The holes for the explosives in the Bingham Canyon Mine are drilled in very precise locations by machines guided by satellites in space.

Bingham Canyon Mine

width: 4 kilometres   depth: 1.2 kilometres

Rock to metal

The mine is worked all year round. First, the ground is shattered by explosives. The rock blown out by the explosives is crushed to a fine powder. The powder is added to tanks of water, where the metal particles float on top and the worthless rock particles, called **gangue**, sink to the bottom. The metal-rich water, called slurry, is sent along a pipe to a smelter. This is a type of furnace where the different ores are melted and separated. The metals are then separated from the ores at the refinery.

▼ *Blasting creates lines of terraces called benches. The benches higher up are set back to stop the walls from collapsing.*

Transporting blast rock

The rock blown out by the explosives is scooped up by mechanical shovels and loaded into giant trucks, which carry it away to be processed. Every day, 408,000 tonnes of rock are removed. The trucks take the rock to a crusher.

▲ *A steady stream of trucks carries rock to the crusher and then returns for more. The biggest of these trucks can carry 290 tonnes of rock.*

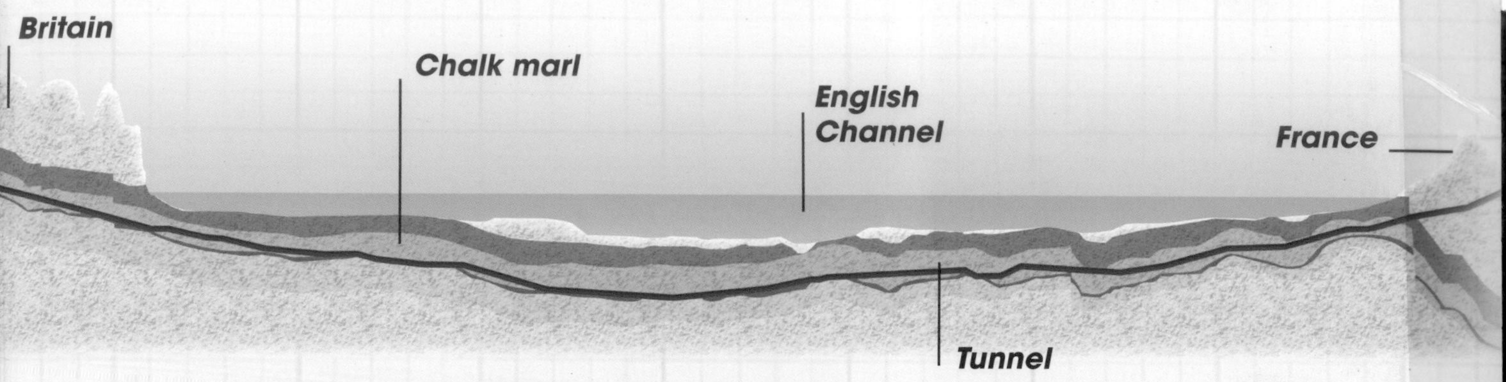

Britain

Chalk marl

English Channel

France

Tunnel

▲ **The Channel Tunnel follows a layer of rock called chalk marl. The tunnel boring machines (TBMs) were steered left, right, up and down to stay within this layer.**

Planning the route

To plan exactly where and how deep the tunnel would have to go, **geologists** needed to know what types of rock were under the seabed and how deep and how thick these layers were. They found this out by setting off small explosions and watching how the sound bounced off the various layers of rock.

◄ **A 450-tonne TBM is lowered down a shaft at Sangatte in France to begin work on the tunnel.**

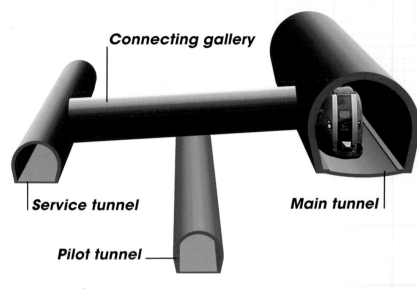

Connecting gallery

Service tunnel

Pilot tunnel

Main tunnel

◄ *The main tunnel is horseshoe-shaped for most of the route, but it is circular in areas with difficult rock formations as this is a stronger shape.*

By the 1960s, the number of people crossing the Tsugaru Strait between the Japanese islands of Honshu and Hokkaido was growing fast. More than 4 million people were crossing by ferry every single year. It was decided to build a tunnel. Construction of the Seikan Tunnel began in 1971. A small **pilot tunnel** was dug first, then a **service tunnel** and finally the rail tunnel through which trains would travel. Two stations were built inside the tunnel. They were the first railway stations ever built under the sea. The Seikan Tunnel opened in 1988.

MEGA FACTS

The Seikan Tunnel is 53.85 kilometres long. Some 23.3 kilometres of this is below the seabed. In places, the tunnel lies 140 metres under the seabed.

The Channel Tunnel runs beneath the English Channel between the UK and France. Construction work began in 1987. The Channel Tunnel is actually three tunnels – two 7.6-metre wide railway tunnels, with a 4.8-metre service tunnel between them. The service tunnel provides access for workers and serves as an escape route in an emergency. The rail tunnels are linked to each other every 250 metres by small tunnels, called piston relief ducts. These let air being pushed along in front of a train escape into the other tunnel.

MEGA FACTS

Every day, 2.5 million readings are taken from 500 sensors inside the Channel Tunnel to make sure that there is no build-up of dangerous gases.

▼ *Specially designed trains run through the Channel Tunnel at up to 160 kilometres per hour.*

3213

eurostar

The Channel Tunnel

total length: 50 kilometres

Boring from each end

Tunnelling was carried out by 11 giant TBMs. Six of them bored the undersea part of the tunnels – three started from each end and headed for the middle. Up to 2400 tonnes of rock was brought out of each end of the tunnel every hour. On the French side, it was mixed with water to form slurry, which was piped across the countryside and poured into a lagoon. On the British side, it was piled up on the shore, where it formed a new piece of land. The machines boring the rail tunnels met in May and June 1991.

▲ **When finished, the Channel Tunnel was 50 kilometres long.**

▲ *The curved lining segments were hoisted into place against the tunnel wall. Cement was pumped behind the segments to fill any small gaps.*

Famous digs

Some of the darkest depths dug or drilled into the Earth's surface are famous because of their history or their great depth. The most famous mines, tunnels and drilled holes include the TauTona Mine, the Holland Tunnel and the Kola Superdeep Borehole.

▲ *Miners walk from one elevator shaft to another on their way to the bottom of the TauTona mine, the world's deepest.*

Record-breaking mine

The TauTona gold mine in South Africa is the world's deepest mine. The lowest part of the mine is 3.9 kilometres underground. Miners working in the lowest level have to take an hour-long journey by lift to reach the surface. The temperature at the bottom of the mine can reach 55 degrees Celsius. Air conditioners take in this air and cool it to 28 degrees Celsius to make it possible for miners to work.

MEGA FACTS

The Holland Tunnel was fitted with 84 ventilation fans – 42 blow in fresh air and 42 suck out stale air. The air in the tunnel is replaced every 90 seconds.

▲ *The Holland Tunnel, which opened in 1927, was the world's first underwater road tunnel. It is 2.6 kilometres long.*

Going superdeep

In the 1970s, scientists in the Soviet Union drilled the deepest hole in the **Earth's crust**. The Kola Superdeep Borehole is 12,262 metres deep. Drilling was stopped in 1992 because the rock at the bottom was too hot. It was 180 degrees Celsius – nearly twice as hot as boiling water. Had they continued drilling down to the target of 15,000 metres, scientists calculated that the temperature would have reached 300 degrees Celsius!

▶ *A special commerative stamp was released in 1987 to celebrate the digging of the Kola Superdeep Borehole.*

The Holland Tunnel

In the early 1900s, ferries crossing the Hudson River between New York and New Jersey were carrying 30 million vehicles a year. It was clear that a permanent link was needed to carry this traffic, so the Holland Tunnel was built. Tests revealed that the carbon monoxide gas given off by car engines was lethal, so fresh air had to be pumped in to clear out the dangerous fumes. The tunnel opened in 1927 and is still in use today.

Drilling

The oil and natural gas that fuel the modern world formed deep underground. They are brought up to the surface by drilling holes in the ground. Scientists drill deep holes in the ground too, to learn more about the Earth and its past.

Oil and gas are found by looking for the right kind of rocks in the ground. Geologists search for two types of rock, called reservoir rocks and cap rocks. Reservoir rocks are porous, which means that they have holes in them. The oil and gas fill the holes, like a sponge full of water. The right sort of rock must also form above the oil and gas to stop them bubbling up to the surface. This cap rock traps the oil and gas underground. When oil and gas are found, a hole is drilled down to them by a metal pipe with a toothed drill bit at the end. The drill is held by a tower called a **derrick**. Once the drilling rig strikes oil or gas, the top of the well is fitted with a series of valves to control the flow of oil or gas.

MEGA FACTS

The deepest ice core was drilled in Antarctica in 1998. It is 3623 metres deep. The deepest ice in the core fell as snow about 420,000 years ago.

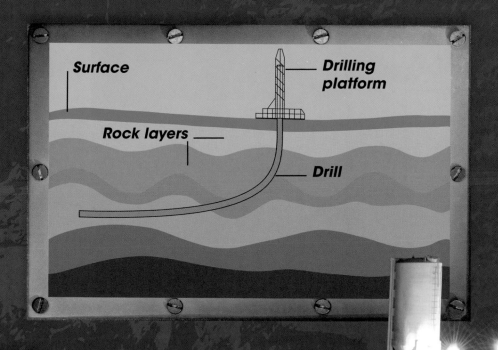

Surface

Drilling platform

Rock layers

Drill

◄ Drills do not have to go straight down. The end of a drill can be steered. This is called directional drilling. It is used where a drilling platform cannot be placed directly above an oil or gas field.

Engine

Ice cores

Holes are drilled through ice with a hollow drill-pipe. When the drill is pulled up, the ice inside the pipe, called an **ice core**, comes up with it. The ice was once snow that fell on the ground. The weight of new snow on top squashed the snow underneath and changed it to solid ice. The deeper the ice, the older it is.

Scientists study ice cores to learn about the climate in the past. The thickness of the layers of ice in the core show how much it snowed every year. Little bits of plants, particles of soot or ash and even bubbles of ancient air trapped in the ice give more clues.

▲ *These scientists are drilling an ice core on a mountain-top in Bolivia. The drill is powered by electricity made by solar panels.*

Derrick

Turntable

◄ *Inside the derrick, a turntable turns the pipe. The pipe turns a tough cutter called a drill bit.*

Thunder Horse is an **oil field** in the Gulf of Mexico. It was discovered in 1999 by a drillship called *Discoverer 534*, and is one of the deepest oil fields ever found.

Drillships search for oil by drilling holes called exploration wells. *Discoverer 534* lowered its drill to the seabed and drilled down 7850 metres before it struck oil. Another drillship, the *Discoveror Enterprise*, drilled a second exploration well and also struck oil. A production platform was brought in to extract the oil. The production platform is called the Thunder Horse PDQ (production drilling quarters). It is a giant structure in which up to 229 people can live and work.

Flame boom

Derrick

Crane

Towing tug

▲ *The* **Discoverer Enterprise** *drilled one of the first wells in the Thunder Horse oil field.*

Thunder Horse Oil Field

water depth: 1844.04 metres

Hurricane damage

Living quarters

Lifeboats

Thunder Horse was due to begin producing oil and gas in 2005. However, the workers had to be taken off the rig because a hurricane was heading for it. When they returned, they found the platform leaning over at an angle. It was repaired quickly, but then cracks were found in pipes at the top of the well on the seabed. As a result, Thunder Horse began producing oil and gas only in 2008.

▲ **The Thunder Horse PDQ was tipped over in July 2005 by Hurricane Dennis.**

Supporting leg

▲ *The Thunder Horse PDQ is built on top of four massive legs that stand on a hull just under the surface of the water.*

MEGA FACTS

The Thunder Horse production platform produces enough oil to power the homes of 80,000 people.

Deep dangers

Deep mines and drill-holes can sometimes damage the land around them. Tunnels can cause problems for the vehicles that travel through them. Compared to the countless trillions of tonnes of rock and earth all around them, mines and drill-holes are tiny pinpricks in the Earth's crust. Even so, they can upset the delicate balance of underground forces.

Making quakes

Deep mines can change underground forces just enough to trigger an earthquake. A geothermal power plant in Basel, Switzerland, was closed down in 2009. It was believed to have triggered an earthquake under the city three years earlier. Coal mining may have triggered the biggest earthquake in Australia's history in Newcastle, New South Wales in 1989.

◀ *Work was stopped at the Deep Heat Mining geothermal experiment in Basel, after injections of high-pressure water triggered a small earthquake.*

▼ *In freezing cold weather, the heat inside a long, deep tunnel, such as the Channel Tunnel, can melt snow on a train.*

The wrong kind of snow

Trains ground to a halt in the Channel Tunnel on 18 December 2009 due to cold temperatures outside the tunnel. Snow was blowing against the trains as they headed towards the French end of the tunnel. The power cars at the front and back of each train have ventilation grilles on each side to let in air for cooling. A sheet of material behind the grille normally stops snow getting through, but the snow on that night was so powdery that it got in. The warm air in the tunnel melted the snow, and the water ran into the electronic systems, which then broke down.

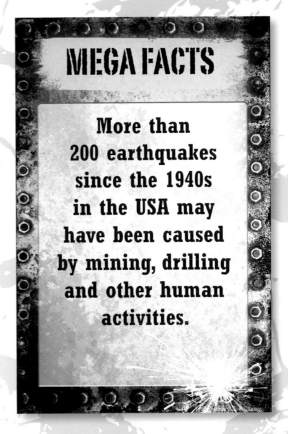

MEGA FACTS

More than 200 earthquakes since the 1940s in the USA may have been caused by mining, drilling and other human activities.

▲ Digging deep holes in the ground, such as this old mine in Alaska, USA, is thought to trigger earthquakes, even in places where earthquakes are rare.

Underground power

Holes drilled in the ground can be used to make electricity. The power stations that do this are called geothermal power stations. They make electricity using heat from deep underground, where volcanic activity can turn water into super-hot steam.

Drilling for heat

To use the heat, holes are drilled at least 3 kilometres deep into the ground. Cold water is pumped down some of the drill-holes. Deep underground, the water soaks up heat from hot rock. If the rock is hot enough, the water changes into steam. The hot water or steam comes back up to the surface through more drill-holes. The heat can be used to heat buildings or to make electricity.

MEGA FACTS

The first geothermal power station was built in Larderello, Italy, in 1904. Today, there are geothermal power stations in 24 countries.

▲ *This geothermal power station in Iceland empties hot water into a nearby lagoon, where people bathe in waters that are at least 37 degrees Celsius all year round.*

Power stations

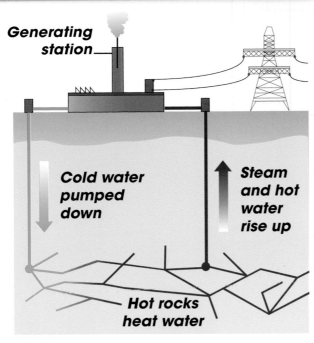

Generating station

Cold water pumped down

Steam and hot water rise up

Hot rocks heat water

To make electricity, steam coming up out of the drill-holes makes drums or wheels called **turbines**, spin very fast. The spinning turbines power generators, which make electricity. If there is not enough heat underground to make steam, the hot water is used to heat a different liquid that turns to a gas at a lower temperature than water.

◄ *Geothermal power stations pump cold water into hot rocks deep underground.*

The Geysers

The biggest group of geothermal power stations in the world is in California, USA, at a place called The Geysers. More than 350 wells have been drilled down to a depth of 3.2 kilometres. Water pumped underground comes back to the surface as steam for making electricity. After the steam has been used, it is not wasted.

The steam is cooled to change it back to water, which is sent underground again to make more steam and more electricity. The 22 geothermal power stations at The Geysers produce enough electricity for more than one million people.

Future digs

The undersea tunnels, deep mines and drill-holes that have been made in the Earth's crust are very ambitious projects but there are even more amazing projects to come in the future. There are plans for undersea tunnels to join Japan and Korea, Europe and Africa, and the USA and Russia. Some future transport links, such as the new Hong Kong–Zhuhai-Macau link, will combine bridges with tunnels.

▶ In the future, cars could drive through underwater tunnels held in place by tethers attached to floating pontoons.

MEGA FACTS

The USA and Russia could be linked by a tunnel under the Bering Strait. Called the TKM-World Link, it would be about 100 kilometres long.

New tunnel projects

A tunnel could be built to link Japan and Korea. At 200 kilometres long, it would be the longest ever transport tunnel. The narrow sea channel between Spain and Morocco could be crossed by a tunnel. Linking Europe and Africa, the tunnel would be about 40 kilometres long and at least 300 metres below sea level. If it is built, it will be the world's deepest undersea tunnel.

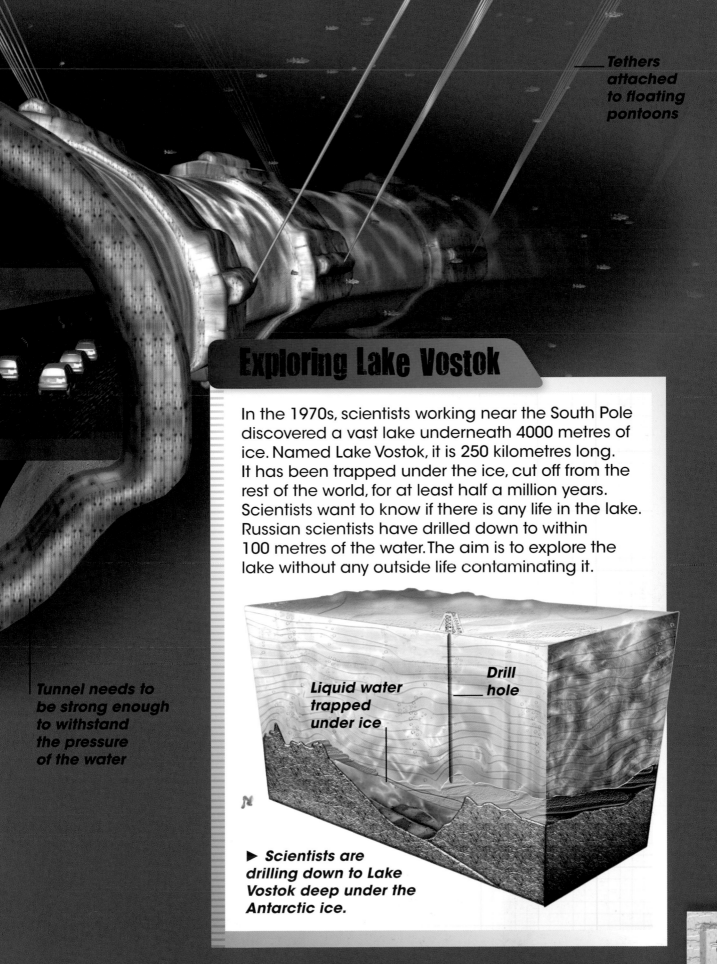

Tethers attached to floating pontoons

Tunnel needs to be strong enough to withstand the pressure of the water

Exploring Lake Vostok

In the 1970s, scientists working near the South Pole discovered a vast lake underneath 4000 metres of ice. Named Lake Vostok, it is 250 kilometres long. It has been trapped under the ice, cut off from the rest of the world, for at least half a million years. Scientists want to know if there is any life in the lake. Russian scientists have drilled down to within 100 metres of the water. The aim is to explore the lake without any outside life contaminating it.

Liquid water trapped under ice

Drill hole

▶ Scientists are drilling down to Lake Vostok deep under the Antarctic ice.

Glossary

blow-out
An accidental, uncontrolled eruption of oil or gas from a well.

derrick
A tower on an oil or gas drilling rig, which is equipped with a crane or hoist for lifting sections of drill pipe into position.

Earth's crust
The outermost layer of the Earth. It is between 5–70 kilometres thick.

fjord
A long, narrow stretch of sea between steep valley sides, carved out by a glacier sliding down to the sea.

gangue
Worthless unwanted rock mixed with a more valuable mineral.

geologist
A scientist who studies rocks.

geothermal gradient
The rising temperature of the Earth at greater depths.

ice core
A cylinder of solid ice that are obtained by drilling down into ice.

mineral
One of the more than 4000 solid chemical substances that form rock.

oil field
An area where oil is found under the ground.

oil well
A hole drilled into the ground to bring up oil from an oil field.

pilot tunnel
A small tunnel that is bored to test the ground where a tunnel is to be dug.

radioactive
Giving out radiation in the form of particles or rays as atoms change from one element to another element. This process is known as radioactive decay and it can be dangerous to humans.

rock burst
A sudden explosion of rock flying out of the wall of a very deep mine, caused by the enormous forces acting on the rock deep underground.

service tunnel
A tunnel that lets workers travel to any part of a road or rail tunnel.

tunnelling shield
A frame or structure that stops a tunnel's walls and roof collapsing while the tunnel is being dug.

turbine
A drum or wheel with blades around the edge. When a liquid or gas hits the blades, the turbine spins. It can be used to power an electricity generator.

ventilated
Replaced stale air or fumes with fresh air.

Type of dig/bore	Name	Location/Depth
1. Deepest borehole	Kola Superdeep Borehole	Russia/12,262 m
2. Deepest oil well	Tiber oil well	Gulf of Mexico/10,683 m
3. Deepest mine	TauTona gold mine	South Africa/3900 m
4. Deepest European metal mine	Pyhäsalmi mine	Finland/1440 m
5. Deepest open-cast mine	Bingham Canyon mine	USA/1200 m
6. Deepest diamond mine	Wesselton mine	South Africa/995 m
7. Deepest undersea tunnel	Eiksund Tunnel	Norway/287 m
8. Deepest rail tunnel	Seikan Tunnel	Japan/240 m
9. Deepest hand-dug hole	The Big Hole diamond mine	South Africa/215 m
10. Deepest subway tunnel	Pyongyang Metro	North Korea/110 m

Take it further

If you could dig or drill a super-deep hole in the ground, where would it be and why would you dig it – to study rock deep underground, to search for gold, or another reason?

Valuable minerals and oil have been found near the North Pole. Some people would like to drill wells and dig mines to reach them. Others think the risk of accidents are too great and these places should be left alone. What do you think?

Most of the electricity we use is made by burning coal or gas. These are both sources of energy from mines and drill-holes. Can you think of any advantages geothermal power stations have over coal-fired or gas-fired power stations?

Useful websites

www.yourdiscovery.com/machines_and_
engineering/tunneltrial/
Dig your own virtual tunnel with this
interactive game.

http://encyclopedia.kids.net.au/page/mi/
Mining
An information-packed website all about
mining.

*Website information is correct at time of going to press. However, the publishers
cannot accept liability for any information or links found on third-party websites.*

Index